The

Self Help

Bible

Volume 1

About Self Esteem

& How to be Confident

Paperback version first published in July 2011 through Lulu

ISBN 978-1-4477-8642-9

My Thanks

Without writing an Oscar acceptance speech, I would like to thank a couple of people who have contributed directly to this book.

For my love of NLP and personal development I must thank Bruce Farrow of Helford 2000. I did all my NLP, Time Line Therapy™ⁱ and Hypnosis training with Bruce and began the most amazing personal journey under his watchful eye, in 2006. He continues to inspire me and I am proud of our continued association. Helford 2000 has gone from strength to strength and Bruce is now one of the most qualified people in the NLP world, both of which are testament to his amazing skill and dedication.

I am also grateful to my partner Julian, for his patience and help in editing this book and to my beautiful children family and friends for sharing and enhancing my journey!

AJB 2011.

This book is dedicated to my Dad,

Michael Robert Ball.

1945 – 2005

Contents   Page No

Contents cont.   Page No

Table of Exercises

What Are The Self Help Bible Books Based on?

I have used my studies of psychology, NLP, Time Line Therapy™ and Hypnosis, my experience of coaching, managing, counselling, parenting and life, as well as the experiences shared with me by my clients, to form the basis of this book.

Where I have mentioned a specific person, I have changed their names and thank them for allowing me to share their experience.

This book has been deliberately structured to allow you to learn in your own way and at your own pace and whilst some of it may be familiar, you may well want to go back to certain bits and that's great.

Each volume will ultimately be available in an audio format, so that you can listen to it as well as read it. There are important benefits to this. Listening uses a different sense to reading, which helps the information to filter through to your unconscious and ensures that you have the tools you need, however you process information best, either by looking or listening.

Exercises are recommended for a minimum of 10 days. This is because, with focus and commitment, this is all it takes to start making real changes in your life; provided you consistently complete the exercise with energy and enthusiasm.

You'll know from the volume on communication if you've read it, that you wipe out most of what is going on around you, so you might find the same things covered in different ways. Again, this helps with the unconscious learning process.

Other things, which are new to you, will challenge your current thinking and feed another of your unconscious desires for new learning. Any time you contemplate something in a different way, you are expanding your horizons and breaking down preconceptions that you have created or accepted.

Just this one simple thing, the contemplation of something new or different, is enough to give you a new perspective and allow you to find the new, better choices available to you right now.

Where appropriate, you will find some (very simple) science. We are fortunate in that studies which began in the 1990's, have really helped to validate much of the theory that NLP put forward in the 1970's.

Doctors are now able to take magnetic images of the brain which show neural pathways and electrical energy, which show visually what is going on in the brain when we think, feel, move etc

Whilst this doesn't necessarily change the processes we use, it does help us to understand why they work. This adds credibility and scientific evidence, to what we know from experience actually works.

If you think you need more science to convince you that this stuff really works, then there are plenty of places you can find that information, but, you may be surprised to find that once you begin asking yourself the right questions and creating better beliefs, that the great results you can create for yourself are proof enough. After all, what better proof of the pudding is there than tasting it for yourself?

If you were faced with the choice of reading about a new super car and taking it for a test drive, you'd rather go for a spin wouldn't you?

So why not allow your mind to believe that any change you want is possible for you now, if you simply accept that it is possible and follow some simple guidelines?

Your best thinking to date has got you to exactly where you are now, so imagine how much better you could be in the future, if you removed some of the obstacles you have unwittingly placed in your way; if you cleared your path ahead and punched a wonderful new destination into your built in Sat Nav.

You were born with the same capabilities and potential as any of the great people you admire, so why not get yourself back on track for the future that has always been there for you?

What's in This Volume?

The purpose of this book is to help answer some simple questions.

- What is Self Esteem?
- What is Self Image?
- Where does Self Esteem come from?
- How can I get better Self Esteem?
- How can I increase my confidence?

Learning how self esteem is created will help you to understand why yours, or that of those around you, may not be as good as you would like.

Increasing self esteem enables a more positive outlook and broadens your horizons.

If you are looking to improve your own self esteem, you will find the explanations and exercises contained in this book, both easy to follow and extremely effective.

If you are a parent or teacher, you will find it an invaluable reminder of how important your role is, in creating good self esteem in children and young people. The exercises can easily be adapted into sessions you could do in a classroom or at home.

How to Get the Most From

The Self Help Bible

Read

The first and most obvious thing is to read them! Start with a title that appeals to you so that you are motivated. This always helps get better results and will give you a chance to see that you like the style of the books and find them easy to follow.

Write things down

If you come to a part which really resonates with you, write it down. There's room in the margins, or better still keep a journal, so that you can look back at it later and see your progress.

When you come to a questions section, write down your answers to that too. It helps clarify things when you have to think about them to write them down.

Only thinking about something allows your mind to drift from one thing to another and you can lose focus without ever really answering the first question, so I'd always recommend writing the question down and then your answer.

Committing something to paper has the added benefit of creating a physical thing from your thoughts, which creates a vibration in tune with that thing. If you understand a little about the universal law of attraction, you will know that what you focus on and create energy about is ultimately what you will attract into your life.

As Napoleon Hill, author of the famous book Think and Grow Rich said

"Thoughts become things!"

Commit

When it comes to the exercises, make sure you follow the instructions carefully and put as much energy into them as you can. Tell yourself that the quality of your future depends on it – because it does! No half measures, no matter how silly it might seem.

Remember you have unconscious patterns (habits) which, although ultimately created for your good, may hold you back and actually sabotage your best efforts. Prevent them from doing so by playing full out every time. No hiding, no lying to yourself, no excuses. Make the time and do it properly!

The more effort you put in, the more benefit you will get out.

My Invitation to You!

Using techniques similar to some of those described in The Self Help Bible series, I have had the privilege of helping people to let go of serious traumas, discard phobias which left them paralysed with fear, or compulsions which threatened to destroy their lives, in a matter of minutes.

I have watched as people unearthed deeply rooted limiting beliefs, which have held them back for almost their entire lives and then transformed them into empowering new beliefs, geared towards success.

I have worked with some fantastic people, who had the one thing necessary to change their lives; the desire to do so.

The Self Help Bible is a growing series, written for anyone who has a genuine desire to help themselves and improve their quality of life.

These concise books will help you to harness the power you possess in your own mind, root out the things which have held you back and find new ways to move forward. They will show you how to reclaim your life and reap the rewards that brings and to become the person you really want to be.

They will give you a start point and explain, in very simple terms, the why and the how. They have been written to show you how inevitable your success is, once you get your unconscious mind to work for you and towards the life that you want.

I hope you will be inspired to better yourself, to seize opportunities and to achieve your true potential.

You are every bit as remarkable, and deserve your success, as much as any other human being on this planet.

It is yours for the taking, with the right mindset, the right system and your willingness to take consistent, focused action.

Every journey begins with a single purposeful step and often the destination is not where we expected it to be. Why not let today be the day you take the first step to a brighter future, in which you are being, having and doing exactly what you want?

Enjoy your journey x

What Is Self Esteem?

Self-esteem is a term you hear bandied around all over the place, and whilst you probably understand that we all have some and that it's better for it to be high than low, do you actually understand exactly what self esteem is and where it comes from?

Self esteem is a fragile thing and a major factor in determining how you do, how you feel, how and even who you are. It is absolutely essential to keep your levels of self esteem as high as possible and there are some really simple ways to do that.

In the most simplistic of terms, this is how you create your self esteem.

You look at other people who you think either have or do something that you would like and make an unconscious measurement of them.

Then you compare yourself to them in the key areas you have identified, using your self-image. The difference you perceive between the two measurements forms your self esteem. The bigger the gap is between the two, between the way you see them and the way you see yourself, the less favourable the comparison. The less favourable the comparison, the lower your self esteem will be.

It is quite literally how you *estimate* yourself to be.

Part of the problem with this is that it is 100% subjective. You are measuring the other person by what you perceive and your perception of yourself will always be skewed, to support the way your beliefs have encouraged you to think.

As little as 50 years ago, although we were beginning to see more of the world thanks to television and magazines etc, we were not yet bombarded by the millions of images of beautiful (airbrushed) people, achieving the most amazing things, often despite incredible odds, that we see today.

Nowadays, we are exposed to such a huge variety of extraordinary people with whom to compare ourselves, it is little wonder that low self esteem seems to be so common. It is far too easy now, to play down our own achievements because we see others doing so much more, or so much better.

You must remember that just because you believe that someone else has done more or better than you, or looks better (in your opinion), or weighs less, or is funnier or more charming or whatever stick you are using to beat yourself with; it doesn't detract from you at all.

You are a magnificent human being, with amazing capacities and capabilities. I bet you are beautiful to at least one person in this world. You are more clever than some, more witty, more compassionate, more hardworking than others.

All that matters is that you believe in you. What anyone else does, has or is, does not matter a jot. Your success or failure depends entirely on you!

How Good is Your Self Esteem?

A quick and easy way to see what your self esteem is like begins by thinking about who your ideal you is.

You might do this by thinking about another person. Someone you really admire, someone you think is beautiful, someone who has achieved things that you would love to achieve, or someone you consider to be a good or clever person.

Or, you may prefer to do this in a more abstract way, by considering the qualities you would like to have, or the things you would like to accomplish.

Or, you may like to think about the things about yourself that you would change and in what way.

However you choose to do it is just fine, as long as you can get a clear idea or picture, of what the ideal you is like.

Exercise 1

What is your current level of Self Esteem?

Take a sheet of paper and divide it into 3 columns, as below

Great Things About the Ideal Me	Current Me Score	Self Esteem Score

1. In the first column, list the aspects of this ideal you that are important. Remember, there are no right or wrong answers. Just write what you feel is important, the things that you pictured in your mind when you thought about how you'd like to be and makes sense to you.

The next thing to do is to compare where you are right now, with the person you would like to become.

Where are the differences?

Are they physical or intellectual?

Are they mainly things constrained by values and beliefs you hold, or emotional issues?

Already this will give you a clue as to where you need to direct your energy and help you to see where you are beating yourself up the most!

2. In the second column, give yourself a score out of 10 for each item in column 1. You get a 10 for

things you think you are already there on and 1 for the things you feel are weakest on.

Now that you have two markers, the ideal you and you as you currently see yourself, you can measure your self esteem. It's basically the gap between the two!

3. Take the number in column 2 away from 10 and put this figure in column 3.

The bigger the number, the farther you perceive yourself being from your ideal.

Again, however you measure and compare them is just fine. This isn't a black and white issue, so whatever answer you give yourself, as long as it is honest, is the right one.

It's really important to remember, that this is only how you see yourself, pick one of the things you dislike about yourself and ask your kids about it, for a different point of view! Or your best friend or partner. I can pretty much guarantee that you will be your own harshest critic.

Now, it doesn't need me to point out, that if your self image, that picture of you as you currently are, is very poor, then the gap between that and your ideal you is going to be huge; and the bigger the gap, the lower your self esteem.

One of the main reasons why it is important to have a good self image, is the role it plays in determining your level of self esteem. Your self esteem is derived from comparing your ideal self, usually made up of bits of people whom you admire, with your self image.

Therefore, if your self image is poor, you will find yourself comparing unfavourably with your ideal you and your self esteem will suffer as a result.

In reality, in order to improve your self esteem, you really need to start with your self image. Let's examine how your self image became what it is today and what you can do to remodel it.

Self Image

What Is Self Image?

In very simple terms, your self image is basically the mental picture that you have created of yourself, the you that exists only in your head! It is made up of a number of elements which fall into two broad groups.

The first group contains the things which others are able to see and which could be objectively investigated, or measured. Things like how tall you are, what colour your eyes are, whether you are male or female and what your IQ is, for example.

The second group consists of the things that you have learned about yourself and is the most important. These are the things which you have come to believe about you, either through personal experience, or more often by your acceptance of other people's judgements and opinions.

This last part is so important, because it forms the basis of many of your beliefs about yourself and the way you think, relate to others, behave and store your experiences and all of these are influenced and filtered by your beliefs.

Improving your self image will require some conscious effort on your part, but the results will make the effort worthwhile. The better your self image, the higher and more stable your self esteem and the higher your self esteem, the more confidence you will have and the more authentic and fulfilling your life will be.

Where Does Your Self Image Come From?

Most of the information you needed to gather, in order to form your self image and many of the beliefs you hold in general, will have been collected when you were still a child. This is a major problem in itself for two key reasons.

Firstly, it means that a lot of the information used will have come from other children, who are not yet equipped to be objective, or think about the impact of their words on others.

Secondly, you did not yet have enough mental competency, to evaluate the input you received from others.

When you add to this the fact that many adults are not consciously aware of the damage they can cause, through a careless choice of words, or the example they set, it is no wonder that many beliefs and values, learned at an early age, do not serve you well if maintained into adulthood.

This in no way implies that any adults caused you any intentional damage, it is however a good reminder, that we need to remember to consider the potential impact of our words and actions at all times, particularly in relation to young people.

If you think about some of the things you believe about yourself, that help to shape your self image, you would probably be surprised to discover, or rather remember, the source of those beliefs.

Perhaps a nickname you had when you were young, or something which was true for a time. How many children, who were once a little chubby, regard themselves as 'fat' all their lives for example, despite the fact that they are no longer the least bit overweight.

How many people label themselves as stupid at an early age and go through life unfulfilled, never achieving their potential, because of that label and the belief they hold about it?

The beliefs you hold about yourself are arguably the most fundamentally important things to you.

If I were to ask you to make an important decision which would shape the rest of your life and either limit you or propel you to success, would you base it on a child's outlook?

Would you ask a 4 year old whether someone is a good person and then base your own opinion on their answer? I imagine you will answer a resounding no to those questions and yet, for many people that's exactly what you have done!

Your Beliefs and Self Esteem

Your beliefs about yourself and your emotions are fundamental to your self esteem. They can be general or global beliefs, such as 'I am good', 'I am useless', or they can be in a specific area 'I believe I am a good cook' or 'I think I am a poor parent'.

These beliefs trigger emotional responses, which seem to validate and reinforce them, which in turn raise or lower your self esteem. When you say them to yourself, or notice something which matches them, you will feel a certain way. Each time you get that same feeling you add a brick to the wall of that belief. If it's a good or empowering belief, your wall will have a staircase in it, that allows you to climb higher as the wall grows and to see over the wall and survey the rest of your life from a positive vantage point.

If it's a negative belief, your wall will just grow taller, keeping you imprisoned behind it, so that 'it' becomes all you can see.

This wall will tower over you and prevent you from seeing opportunities when they appear. You will live in its shadow and it will taint every aspect of your life it encroaches on.

For example, you believe you are a good cook and thinking that makes you feel good. You cook something well and you experience a sense of triumph and feel pleased with yourself, which confirms your belief about your cooking ability.

Both of these positive things contribute to your self esteem because you measure up well to your view of yourself as a good cook. Furthermore, because your unconscious loves to find links and similarities between things, this belief will also increase your bank of positive feelings and beliefs about yourself. A bit like ink bleeds on wet blotting paper, the fact that you believe you can do one thing well will lead you to believe you might be able to do other things well too.

Amazingly, even if you don't always cook well, your fundamental belief that you are a good cook, will usually override the times when you're not as successful and your belief and self esteem remain intact. That's part of the magic of positive beliefs and the power of your unconscious mind.

In the same way, if you perceive yourself to have a weakness in a particular area and something happens which seems to confirm that, your belief gets stronger and your self esteem drops.

So you believe you are a poor parent, your teenage child tells you she hates you and your belief is reinforced. Not good for your self esteem.

Unfortunately, even if you do something which appears to contradict this belief, your unconscious mind is likely to ignore the 'unusual´ success, as it doesn't fit in with your belief about yourself.

Your unconscious is always on your side and will look for ways to support your beliefs. You will generally notice things which fit in with and confirm your beliefs, rather than things which go against them.

There is of course an obvious problem with that. If your beliefs are not positive in the first place, your poor old unconscious will still work hard to protect them and promote them for you. It's not a flaw, just the way our minds are programmed to work and once you understand that, you can make it work for you.

The best way to raise your self esteem and improve your confidence, is to work on your self image and your beliefs about yourself. Your beliefs are fundamental to the way your unconscious mind processes all the information it receives, about you and your existence. You need to work out which of your beliefs about yourself are serving you and promote them. The ones that aren't helpful, you need to change!

Why would you want to keep believing things which don't make you feel good or don't help you?

It's like having the choice between two cars for a long journey. Do you choose the one which is well serviced, has a sound engine and you know will get you there safely and comfortably? Or, do you pick the one which breaks down regularly, hasn't been maintained and is unlikely to last the distance?

When put like that, the answer is quite blatant isn't it!

Where Did Your Beliefs Come From?

There will be things you believe, that were I to suggest they may not be true, you would be horrified! Wars are consistently fought and lost on matters of principle, which are really just a clash of strong beliefs. Obviously my intent in writing this book is not to offend you, I would however like to make you think a little!

What if I could show you that everything you believe is only true for you because you decided it is?

You have effectively built your life around a set of rules, given to you by someone else, which you at some point decided to accept as your own – often without even questioning!

Let's go right back to when you were born. You were, like every other baby, a blank canvas. You didn't know or believe anything.

The people around you, who shared your life, had their own sets of beliefs and you experienced these through your interactions with them. Your family, your peers, your teachers, all those who shared your days, consistently showed you and told you what was right and wrong, good and bad, true and untrue through their words and actions.

You soaked up all this information like a sponge and from very early on began to accept and reject what they showed you, to create your own set of beliefs and values.

The key thing to understand here, is that all these things are only true because people, you included, decided they were.

I am not talking about scientific or mathematical provable facts here, nothing as trivial as that! These are the truths around which you have built your life.

It's a little like weeds and flowers. Who decides what is a weed and what is a flower?

My youngest son has planted some seeds this year designed to attract butterflies. As they have grown, I recognise a number of plants that would conventionally be classed as weeds amongst them. In this context however, they are plants to attract butterflies and therefore have a rightful place in my flower border.

So in many ways, like the weeds in the garden, our beliefs are given meaning by their context. A key thing here is that contexts change. What might have been right for your mother a generation ago, is not necessarily right for you. Similarly, what was right for you in your life 10 years ago, may not be the best option for you now.

Rather than viewing your beliefs as a series of rigid commandments, which are black and white and set for life; see them instead as a support network for your well being. A set of guidelines to offer direction, enabling you to become the best possible version of yourself.

Of course, on top of the input from all the people you encounter, the media and the virtual world play a bigger and bigger part in your life and in influencing your beliefs.

Put anything into Google and you will get thousands if not millions of 'expert opinions' and 'truths' about what you are looking for. Almost all of what you will see is only based on what someone else believes to be true. It may be for them but that doesn't mean it has to be for you.

A psychopath may believe he is justified in killing any woman that resembles his mother. Most of us would not agree.

Many of us would however, understand a parent feeling that way about someone who hurt their child. It's all about context and our beliefs.

Think for a moment about the television and the things you watch regularly. Most of the soaps which are so popular nowadays, are just regular instalments of doom and gloom! Run through the last 5 big storylines in any soap you watch and I bet you they are not happy ones! Whilst this may on the one hand make you feel glad you are not living the lives of those on screen characters, it also speaks volumes to you unconsciously.

Your unconscious mind does not differentiate between the real and the imagined. That's why dreams feel so real and why rehearsal is such a powerful tool.

It (your unconscious mind that is) also takes everything personally. You are effectively absorbing all that negativity and processing those negative emotions as if they were your own! Why would you do that to yourself on a regular basis? You are conditioning yourself in the most basic way, like one of Pavlov's dogs, to expect misery and lack in your life. That influences your beliefs and limits your expectations and often you end up getting exactly what you thought you would!

Even the news and so called factual journalism is not without bias. Just watch the same story on different channels to see that. Just about all the information you get is second hand, filtered first through the belief system of someone else.

EXERCISE 2

What are you watching?

If you regularly watch certain programmes on TV, keep a diary for a couple of weeks.

1. Rate your mood before you watch the episode – nothing difficult, use a simple 1 to 5 scoring or smiley faces or a couple of adjectives, whatever works for you –

2. Then rate it again after the programme and compare the two.

You may be surprised to find that you feel noticeably less positive after the programme.

3. Watch a funny movie or something genuinely uplifting and rate your mood before and after.

4. Compare the changes caused by each of the two types of programme and notice the difference.

What you do next is up to you. You may benefit from changing what you watch or reducing the amount of TV you watch altogether. Only you can decide that!

I used to watch lots of sad films. I'd get a film, a glass of wine and a box of tissues, have a damn good cry and believe I was enjoying myself! My perception was that having a good cry made me feel better.

I stopped doing that when I got to a period of my life where I was so low the tears came without the film and I had enough misery of my own not to need anyone else's!

We all know what a wonderful thing hindsight is and looking back I can see that the films I was watching, actually mirrored the deep sadness that was in my life at the time and which I wasn't ready to face up to.

Instead of dealing with my own pain, I cried for the people in the films and whilst the tears gave me a kind of release, it did nothing to help solve my issues.

A couple of years on and I barely watch TV now. When I do, I am much more discerning. I think about my frame of mind and question why I would watch a certain programme before I switch on. No more watching sick children in hospital, dreary soaps or things which make me angry. Why would I? Instead I read, or write or watch something which makes me think in a constructive or uplifting way.

The difference this change has made is tangible. On the odd occasion I fancy a bit of what I call 'Mindless TV' and I catch a bit of one of the soaps I followed for years. I find now it's a bit like third party viewing. Instead of empathising with the characters and being drawn in, I find the whole thing laughable and sad. It never takes long to work out what I've missed, even if it's been years since I watched, which speaks volumes in itself!

If you notice during the exercise above that your mood is adversely affected by what you watch on TV, try something radical. Like the off switch!

Papers are another great source of misery and I've stopped reading those too. Whilst out shopping a few weeks ago, my eldest son called out 'Look Mum, have you seen that story about a baby being put in a washing machine?'

'No! Why would I want to?' I replied! You might think I am deluding myself and just avoiding the harsh realities of the world today, but my question would always be the same, 'For what purpose?' If you can give me one good reason why I should read that kind of thing I might think about it!

If, on the other hand, I can write a book, that will make one person think about themselves and make a positive change in their lives, then I think that is a much better use of my time!

Helpful Beliefs

Some of the beliefs you hold will stand you in good stead and help you in life. Some are unique to you and others are more commonplace beliefs, designed to enable us to live in dense populations in a reasonable, peaceful way. Things like 'It's wrong to steal' or 'What goes around comes around' for example are widely held beliefs, considered by many people to be true.

Many of the regulations which hold society together are only possible because we are taught to believe we should obey the rules of society.

We park, smoke, eat, walk and travel where we are told to for example and though the threat of a financial fine might well put us off, most of us follow these rules because we have been conditioned to hold the belief that we should- We do as we're told!

If you are a parent, you have probably felt annoyed when you've seen someone without a child parking in the space designated for 'parent and toddler?' Yet if you think about it, all this person is really doing, is not adhering to one of our society's little rules because they don't believe they have to! He or she isn't doing it to deliberately upset you, spoil your day, or to make you angry. They just don't see why they can't park there, or they believe they have as valid a reason to park there as you!

In the same way you may also hold beliefs about yourself which are helpful to you. Positive thoughts and feelings about parts of yourself that you like, or things you feel you are good at. These may have been created without you even realising it, unconsciously, or you might have deliberately created them through some form of self development. If you are fortunate they will have been helped by positive or thoughtful people when you were a child.

Unhelpful Beliefs and How to Change Them

Unfortunately, most of us also hold unhelpful or limiting beliefs about ourselves. These might be thoughts about how you look, how intelligent you are, what you can expect to achieve, what you deserve to have, do or be.

Some are lightly held beliefs which may crop up from time to time, others are so fundamental to you that they will influence everything you do and think. A bit like a veil between you and the world. Everything you see will be masked or blurred by the veil.

The most important message of all where beliefs are concerned links back to the start of this chapter.

You were born without any of the beliefs that you now hold. In other words you have learned them.

More often than not we accept these thoughts into our belief library at an unconscious level, completely oblivious to the fact that we didn't hold them before, or that they are not actually true.

Beliefs are only true if you allow them, or want them, to be.

Anything you have learned you can change!

If you change the things you believe about yourself, you will change the way you feel about, see and value yourself and so increase your self esteem and self confidence.

There are some really simple techniques I have developed and used to great effect. You can do as little or as much as you can make time for, as long as you do something and do it consistently, you will have a positive effect.

Exercise 3

Assess your beliefs

1. Make a table with 3 columns in (you can download a free template from my website for this http://julianandamanda.com)

2. Label column 1, *Positive Things I Believe About Myself*.

Label column 2, *Negative Things I Believe About Myself.*

Label the third column *Evidence*, as shown below

Positive Things I Believe About Myself	Negative Things I Believe About Myself	Evidence

3. In column 1 write down all the positive things you believe about yourself and your life. Write as many as you can, at least 50.

4. In column 2 list all the negative or unhelpful things you believe about yourself and your life. Write as many as you can, at least 50.

In just doing this you will already begin to see which way your beliefs tend to function and if there is an imbalance in your life.

Are they mostly helpful and supportive beliefs or mostly unhelpful and limiting? You can see this by looking at which column is fullest and which was the easiest to complete.

What does this tell you?

Imagine for a moment that none of them were true. What difference would that make to your life?

Imagine that you could change the unhelpful ones right now, what would you prefer them to be?

5. Start with the thing you believe most strongly in column 1, and list, in the third column, at least 3 things which support and prove this belief to be true. If you don't have much time you could pick just a couple a day and work your way through the list.

6. For each of the things you list in column 2, you must write at least 3 examples of things which go against or disprove this belief in column 3. Again, pick the most firmly held beliefs first.

7. Pick two or three really key beliefs that you would love to change now. Every day for 10 days make an effort to consciously notice the things which you do, say and think which either:

a) reinforce or back up the positive things you believe about yourself

or

b) undermine or go against the things listed in column 2 unhelpful beliefs

8.   Write down what you notice in your Evidence column

When you find that you are consistently spotting the things you do which make the unhelpful beliefs stronger, start challenging yourself.

Stop the thoughts in your head and replace them with more positive ones.

If you find it hard to completely turn those thoughts around to start with, you might go from a thought like *'I can't do it'* to *'I might struggle but I will do this'* or *'I'll need help to do this'* and that's fine. Rome wasn't built in a day!

As time goes by make your challenges to yourself harder. Make the new statements stronger and even more positive. Push yourself to think great things about yourself even if you don't yet believe them.

Once you find you can think great things about yourself without feeling anything negative – in other words when you can say them comfortably – go back to your first list and see which beliefs you no longer hold about yourself. Read them to yourself and you'll be surprised that some of them will just seem silly!

Keep going until you no longer hold unhelpful beliefs about yourself at all!

If you are consistent in the amount and intensity of the effort you put into this activity, it only takes about 10 days to install a new behaviour, or change a belief and replace it with a new one. So get cracking with that list and change the way you behave and think about yourself.

Remember, your beliefs are your business. You can choose to believe whatever you like so why would you pick anything except great things which serve you well?

You don't have to accept anyone else's beliefs as your own. They may have been right for you once but there may be some that are even better for you now.

If you would like more self development information and tools, be sure to check out the personal development section on our web site, http://julianandamanda.com

Another Really Easy Way to Boost Your Self Esteem Quickly!

Self Esteem is one of the most basic ways in which you measure and value yourself and decides how you live your life and interact with other people.

It is an underlying part of your every decision, feeling and response and the level of your self esteem affects how you live and what you strive for, which in turn contributes to your overall satisfaction and happiness in life.

Having a good level of self esteem will enable you to form healthy relationships and to treat others with fairness and respect.

We tend to accept the things that fit in with our way of thinking and ignore those that do not. This is fine in a positive scenario, but can be both limiting and damaging, if the influence is a negative one.

If you constantly doubt and measure yourself badly against others, you will not feel good. Also, if you put other people down all the time, finding fault in their beliefs or behaviour, it shows that you are very far from liking yourself - It can be a way for the mind to ignore the fact that your own behaviour is similarly bad.

Many of us look to others, to tell us that we're doing ok and don't value or believe in our own judgements.

Imagine then how empowering it would be, instead of basing how you see yourself on the opinion of others, to have the self confidence to make decisions and move forward freely in your life, without the constant need for approval.

So, once you recognise the importance and value of having good self esteem, you can do something about changing it and one of the best ways to improve how we feel about ourselves, is through self education.

To do this, you first have to be able to trust and value your own abilities and having achieved that, no one else will be able to make you feel that your decisions and feelings are wrong, or inferior to theirs.

If you can imagine what it would be like to appreciate and like yourself, then you can do it. Take control of your own life, thoughts and feelings, and you will find yourself empowered and able to face and even benefit from, situations, decisions and people that you may have previously avoided.

As with every journey, self help begins with one step. All you have to do is to want to change and an easy way to begin to build your self esteem and confidence, is by just following this method;

Exercise 4

Recognise Your Achievements

1. Every night for 10 days, write for at least five minutes, a list of things that you have achieved in your life to date. These can be from the smallest and oldest of your achievements, like learning to count or tie your shoelaces, to big things, such as a time when you managed to do something that you had thought impossible; run a mile, drive a car or motorbike, even baking a cake that was edible!

By the time you get to the end of the ten days, you should have a real mixture of achievements, things that you have managed to do and a long list.

2. Study your list and be pleased with yourself.

3. Then, for the next ten days, write down a minimum of 5 things that you like about yourself; perhaps you are quick to offer help to others, or are conscientious in your work, anything that you can think of really.

Again, by the end of the ten days, you will have another list.

4. Study them both and realise as you look at the hard evidence, that you are in fact a great person, who is able to achieve things.

5. Write down something new that could be added to either list, every day. By combining these three things and reading them back to yourself, you will begin to feel more positive about yourself, able and even assertive, in your everyday life.

It seems simple and it is, things don't have to be difficult to work! It's just learning a different way of looking at things, which allows you to see the real possibilities that lie within yourself.

Become Your Best Friend!

Think about your best friend. They're no more perfect than you are and yet you love them just the same.

Imagine them making a mistake, an error of judgement or doing something silly. You'd forgive them wouldn't you? You may not even get angry at them and I bet that if you did, it wouldn't last long.

Would you go on at them about it for weeks, reminding them at every possible opportunity how stupid it was, or they are?

Would you punish them by making them overeat, even though they want to lose weight?

Or deny them things they enjoy, to teach them a lesson?

Chances are, if you did, they wouldn't be your best friend for long!

It sounds silly when you see it written down and yet this is exactly the kind of thing we do to ourselves all the time! Trouble is, that unlike a friend who you can choose to distance yourself from, you're stuck with yourself!

What has this got to do with anything you ask? Well, it's very simple;

Your unconscious mind; the part of you that runs your body for you, stores all your memories, protects and heals you and controls your emotion; is like a young child. It's listening in all the time to what goes on around you and inside you; and it takes everything very personally. Every time you put yourself down, or beat yourself up, your unconscious mind is listening in and taking offence.

Start treating yourself as though you were your own best friend, because ultimately you are the only person you can count on 100% and the only one who will be with you 24 hours a day, every day of your life.

Exercise 5

STOP!

Do you ever catch yourself, way down a path of negative thought, contemplating something horrid and don't know how you got there? Or do you ever feel that you don't control the thoughts running through your mind?

Sam*[1] is a very successful lawyer but she used to find herself tied in knots, trying to answer questions like which of her two children she loved the most; or who she'd choose if she had to pick a member of her family to be shot. This would lead to anxiety or panic attacks and dreadful feelings of guilt and depression.

I learnt the following technique from Joseph McClendon III and taught it to Sam and within a fortnight she had these black thought paths licked.

Try this the next time you feel that familiar negativity..

1. **Take a deep breath and Shout STOP** – in your head if you can't do it out loud, but out loud is better!

2. **Move your body**. Jump up if you are sitting down and shake your arms as though you are shaking out the feeling. This breaks the cycle and distracts the conscious mind, which is all you need to access the unconscious.

3. Now **squeeze your fist** triumphantly and **shout 'YES'**.

---

[1] Not her real name

4.   Pat yourself on the back and SMILE!

Patting yourself signals reward to your unconscious and starts the formation of a new neural pathway to replace the way you used to react.

5.   Repeat this procedure until the feelings have subsided **or at least 10 times**. You will find that it very quickly becomes difficult to bring back the negative feeling.

Whilst this technique might sound a little odd, it really does work!

What this is doing, is creating the physical, chemical and emotional state associated with a successful scenario where you feel in control and not anxious.

You can use this technique for any negative emotion that causes you problems.

Kill the Monster Before it Grows!

You don't need to wait for the emotion to occur for real either. You can do it in advance so that you kill the feeling off before it even arises! Why give the monster time to grow big? Squash it while it's small!

1.   Sit in a chair and allow yourself briefly to imagine a scenario which triggers the negative feeling. Don't dwell or go into great detail, just enough to get the feeling of it.

2.   As soon as you get the right feeling, take a deep breath, shout STOP and jump up.

3. Move your body and shake your arms, as though you are shaking the emotion out of you.

4. Squeeze your fist or pat yourself on the back (yes literally!) say 'YES' and smile!

5. Sit down and repeat another 9 times. Do this twice a day for 10 days and I promise that you will notice a vast improvement – as long as you do it with serious intent!

Yes you might look a bit silly! So do it when no-one else is around!

What you are doing here is firstly breaking a pattern and then forging a new one.

You have created strong links and pathways in your brain which lead you to feel the negative emotion without even trying. Shouting stop is a verbal command to your unconscious; moving your body breaks the cycle and distracts your conscious mind, which then allows you to replace the negative feeling with a more positive one. You'll very soon find it hard to 'do' that old emotion without slipping straight into the positive one.

Kids are really great at this game by the way, so if you have a little one who is struggling to master things like frustration, play this game with them.

Exercises 6-10

Quick and Easy Ways to Boost Low Self Esteem Daily

1. Speak to yourself – and that means inside your head too – as though you were your own best friend. When things go wrong, learn how to get it right next time and move on. You wouldn't shout at a toddler for falling over would you? Of course not. So, don't dwell on the mistake, focus on a successful outcome next time.

2. When you look at yourself, look for the positive things, instead of noticing every little flaw, and if you see something that isn't as good as it could be, think about it as you would say it to a friend. Be kind to yourself.

3. Find things you like about yourself and notice them out loud (you can do it when you're on your own so you won't feel silly!)

4. Praise yourself when you do something well. If you really want to make this powerful, combine a verbal congratulation with a physical gesture, like patting yourself on the back or squeezing your thumb and first finger together, or squeezing your fist. This creates a link in your brain between the feelings you associate with praise and the physical thing you do – in other words an anchor.

5. As well as praising the good things you do, and anchoring them, you can create what's called a Resource Anchor.

All you have to do for this is to repeat the action you chose for number 4 above, let's say squeezing your fist as that's easy to do anywhere, at any time you feel a strong positive emotion. Try to do it when the emotion is at is strongest and just squeeze - when you are helpless with laughter for example. Do this as often as you can.

> Then, when you are in a negative frame of mind, you can bring back the positive feelings simply by squeezing your fist again. The repeated action will fire the same neurons that were being fired when you were positive and bring back those great feelings. How cool is that!

It shouldn't be too much of a stretch for you to fit these simple steps into your daily routine. I guarantee however, that if you do all of the above, with energy and commitment, for 10 days, you will have installed a set of really beneficial habits in yourself and you will feel better.

Once you have mastered these easy steps, you can begin to add to them and really build your self esteem.

Then, you can concentrate on your goals and the steps that you can take to move towards them and become that ideal you; developing your focus and recognising the opportunities that will occur with increasing frequency, as you attune your mind to be open and seek them.

The Benefits of Using Positive Self-Talk

One of the biggest influences that you can use to your advantage in life is you! In particular, you can use your thoughts and your self-talk (that voice that constantly chats in your head) because they influence your feelings and therefore can have a profound effect on how you deal with life in general.

Unless you have trained yourself to have a quiet mind, through meditation for example, your mind is never quiet. Even while you sleep there are thoughts going through your head as you dream. So, being as you are going to keep talking to yourself no matter what, surely it makes sense to say empowering, positive things to yourself!

By learning to control your self-talk and turning it into positive self-talk rather than negative, which most people do unconsciously throughout the day, you can begin to gain more control over every aspect of your life and make essential changes and better choices.

Your ability to succeed in life largely depends on how you deal with life. A positive mental attitude leads to a confident and ultimately more successful person than one full of negativity. That usually leads to a lack of self-confidence and low self-esteem.

By taking a positive attitude, you look at life in a different way to someone who has a negative attitude. A positive attitude leads to seeing good in people and the world in general, which leads to optimism and success.

Your quality of life is based on how you think and feel from moment to moment and changing the way you think, can drastically change how you see and deal with life.

If you go through life optimistically with a positive attitude, you will be able to deal with life and the problems it sometimes throws at you much better. You will bounce back and recover from problems or set-backs more quickly.

Being more optimistic, you will see the problem for what it is, nothing but a temporary set-back which you can overcome and move on from. When looking at life in this optimistic way you are able to take full control over your thoughts and feelings and turn a negative situation into a more positive one by simply altering the way you think.

Since thoughts can either be positive or negative and you can only have one thought in mind at any one time, then opting for positive will keep your thoughts, feelings and actions optimistic, which creates a happier person who is able to achieve goals much easier.

Remember, you don't have to actually believe these positive things to start with. Just pick things you would like to believe about yourself and with practice they will become real for you.

Using Positive Self-Talk In Your Daily Life

You may well have established a pattern of negative thinking for many years and this will take time to overcome. As with anything, the more effort you put in, the quicker the transformation will be and the sooner you'll see results.

Having a positive attitude is arguably the key to being happy and leading a successful life. Your thoughts play a huge role in how you feel and positive thinking leads to a confident, happy person, while negativity leads to low self-esteem and missing out on so much in life.

We so often talk ourselves out of things without even realising we are doing so. Every day, hundreds of negative thoughts drift freely through our mind; we put ourselves down too much and sow the seeds of self doubt.

There is a small simple tool that you can use throughout the day, to help you to change these negative thoughts and instil a more positive way of thinking. Using daily positive affirmations can change your life drastically for the better. They can make you more confident, more self-aware, more sure of yourself and change your life in many aspects for the better.

In order to establish a new thinking pattern, you need to use positive self-talk throughout the day. Positive self-talk can be used for many different aspects in your life. It can help you to overcome difficult situations, gain more confidence in yourself, help you to quit habits, recover quicker from illness or make changes to your life in general.

Never underestimate the power of positive thinking and self-talk, or of repetition. Most issues you have with self esteem have only come about because you, or someone around you, put you down, discredited or spoke negatively to you repeatedly and you accepted these words as truths, and brought them to life through your thoughts and actions. You can just as easily kill them off and create shiny new, empowering beliefs with words.

To start with you should aim to repeat positive affirmations around 50 times throughout the day.

What Are Positive Affirmations?

Affirmations are just meaningful phrases that you repeat to yourself, on purpose, over and over. This simple technique changes the negative self-talk that you are rarely even aware of doing. It encourages you to look at your life with a more positive attitude.

Positive affirmations can be used throughout the day anywhere and at anytime you need them. The more you use them, the easier it will be for positive thoughts to replace negative ones and you will soon see more positive things happening in your life.

Most of us have for many years bombarded ourselves with negative thoughts, so changing your thoughts and the way you think won't happen overnight. However, if you stick with affirmations they will work, once you have retrained your way of thinking.

Making your affirmations out loud is more beneficial, as it gives more energy to the thought and allows you to hear it too. This helps with unconscious learning and you will find it easier to recall something you have said out loud, than something you have only said in your head.

Below are some examples of phrases or sentences that can be used in positive self-talk to get you going. You can find more examples in downloadable lists on my web site.

Think about and start to notice times when you resort to doubtful or negative thoughts and plan positive antidote phrases in advance. Write them down in your journal too, this will help you to bring them to mind when you need them. Adapt my phrases into your own language to begin with, until you feel confident to start your own from scratch.

✓ *I have an interesting challenge facing me*

This could be used when a problem occurs or you come up against some difficulty. Rather than looking at the situation in a negative way and thinking you have a problem, seeing it as a challenge is a much more positive way of dealing with it. View it as a chance to learn something and as you go, notice what you learn so that you can apply the learnings in the future.

Remember if you can't go through the wall, look for another way over or round it.

No matter what you do in life, even when things seem to go really badly, if you can learn something, you have not failed!

✓ *I like the person I am*

This could be used to bolster self-confidence and gain respect about yourself and the person you are.

Similar statements could be

- o *I am the best*
- o *I am a good person*
- o *I have many excellent qualities*

✓ *I know I can do this*

This could be used if you are faced with a certain task that you would previously have thought you couldn't achieve.

Similarly you could say

- o *I have the ability to conquer this*
- o *I will find the solution to this*

✓ *I am full of health, energy and vitality*

This can be used to encourage good feelings about your health, either after you have been sick or while recovering from an illness.

✓ *I am fulfilled as a person*
✓ *I am happy with my life*

These can be used to encourage good general positive thoughts about yourself

Be careful what you think about others too. If you are the kind of person who spots the flaws in people, notices untidy hair, excess midriff, ill fitting clothes etc STOP!

Every time you think an unkind, spiteful or critical thought about someone else, your unconscious mind is listening and takes it you are referring to yourself!

Next time you notice something, say to that person

✓ *I love you*

Instead, you only need to say it in your head and it will do you the world of good!

Exercises 11 – 15

More Tricks for Beating Low Self Esteem.

There are many other techniques for dealing with low self esteem and I have listed some of my favourites below. Try different ones out to see which suit you best. Expect them to feel a bit odd at first, but persist with them anyway. The benefits of changing your self-talk are so great that it's well worth a few red cheeks and feeling a bit uncomfortable for!

The Mirror Technique

This technique will really help you to appreciate yourself and develop self-awareness and self-esteem. Stand in front of a mirror, preferably a full length one in either just your underwear or better still naked.

Start at your head and work down your body, saying out loud what it is that you like about each part of your body.

For example you could say "I like the way my hair shines, the slight differences in colour where the light hits it," or " my eyes are a lovely shade of _ _ _ _. They sparkle and glint;" or "my eyes are a wonderful feature."

Take the time to go slowly over all your body building up a more positive image of yourself.

Though it might feel silly at first; it will get easier with practice.

The Volume Technique

This technique can be used wherever and whenever you catch yourself thinking a negative thought. As soon as you realise you are having a negative thought, or heading down a path in your mind which will not take you to a happy place, imagine turning down a volume knob inside your head. Turn it down low enough so that you can't hear it any more. Then choose one of your prepared positive affirmations to replace the negative one and turn the volume back up, repeating it to yourself with a big smile on your face.

The Trashcan or Rubbish Bin Technique

If you have repeated negative thoughts, write them down on a scrap of paper, screw the paper up into a ball and throw it into the bin. By doing this you are telling yourself these thoughts are nothing but rubbish and that's where they belong. It's a great symbolic gesture, which is satisfying in itself and sends a very clear message to your unconscious too. If you want to take it one step further, you might like to try a little trick I discovered when I was at University.

I saved crockery that was chipped (and on occasion even bought old plates at jumble sales!) wrote down the things that were troubling me on them and then smashed them! I found it really cathartic to hurl the plates and cups and jump up and down on the bits! It might sound silly and I suppose on one level it is, but it sure worked for me and I always ended up laughing!

The Worry Box

This is similar to the Trash Can, except that this time you write your worries down and put the paper in a special box. This is a great one for children who enjoy the ceremony and the feeling of actually doing something.

You can include both pointless worries and things you need to resolve and leave them in the box until you are ready to deal with them, or bin them. This gives your mind permission not to be concerned with them, leaving you mental space to think about other things or look for a solution.

The Meditation Technique

Find somewhere quiet where you able to relax for 5 or 10 minutes. Close your eyes and let your mind empty of all thoughts and feelings. Begin to repeat your affirmation to yourself over and over again, concentrating on the words you are repeating and believe in what you are saying.

Simple Strategies for a More Positive Life

Mind Your Language!

Listen to yourself and think about what you think about and how you think about it! In other words, watch your words...

If you are constantly thinking spiteful thoughts about other people, noticing their faults and putting them down – either out loud or in your head – you may just as well be saying all those horrible things to yourself. Your unconscious does not differentiate between what you think or say about others and what you think or say about yourself.

It takes it all personally and feels hurt, dejected and sad.

Think and say kind things to others, appreciate and be supportive of them and not only will you feel better because your frame of mind is more positive, you will be making a healthy contribution to their self esteem and that will also reflect on you.

Avoid Mood Hoovers!

You know that person that drains your energy, the one that makes your heart sink when you think about having to speak to or see them? They are a mood hoover!

They might well be very nice people, but their outlook is bleak and being in their company is not good for you. It's like standing in a draught - you will catch cold eventually.

Choose who you people your life with. When making new acquaintances, think of it like you would when you shop. Choose ones who will suit your new, more positive way of being.

Think about who you currently spend your time with. You won't be able to avoid them all, but where possible, reduce the time you spend in the company of energy vampires.

Those you can't avoid, you still have choices. You can either, gently, show them that there are more positive ways to see things, by offering a different viewpoint, or simply being more positive in yourself and hoping it rubs off. You might give them their own copy of this book for example ☺ You can also train yourself to be less susceptible to their behaviour.

One of my coaching clients Michael*[2] had terrible trouble coping with a work colleague who was always very negative, and in fact downright miserable. It was affecting him quite badly, to the point that he arranged his working day to avoid this person, which in turn meant getting home later, which his wife hated. He felt if he didn't do this though, he'd feel so depressed by this other person that he'd take it out at home.

We talked about why this person might be so negative and tried to imagine how life looked through her eyes. This helped from an empathetic perspective, Michael could imagine how it felt to be her, but it didn't make being in her company any more bearable.

We then did an exercise where Michael imagined that he had a magic cloak with a big hood, covered in mirrors.

---

[2] Not his real name

When this lady came near, he saw himself pull this cloak around him so that nothing could reach him and the mirrors would bounce all her energy right back at her.

We ran through various scenarios together, situations that he might encounter at work, so that the next time they met, it was as though he'd done it before.

This worked brilliantly! Not only did Michael deal with their encounters better because he felt in control and empowered, he was also imagining a positive outcome before he went into the situation and therefore was much more likely to get one.

The unconscious loves familiarity and can't tell the difference between something you make up in your head and something that's real, so visualisation and rehearsal can be very powerful tools.

He was able to be more positive towards this lady, who, as will usually be the case eventually, responded by being more positive too. They were never going to be friends but that wasn't the solution Michael was looking for.

The removal of this stress allowed him more time to focus on his work, which led to a promotion. He was able to change his working hours and get home at a more mutually acceptable time for his wife and people in and out of work commented that he seemed happier and more relaxed. Not bad results for an invisible cloak!

Copy the Winners.

When we are young, we are quite happy to look up to other people and try to be like them. Then for some reason, with adulthood comes the notion that we should know it all now and 'just be ourselves.'

Well, what if I were to tell you that the most successful people on the planet are just people like you and I and most of them dedicate some time to their ongoing development. Look at how coaching has grown as an industry in the past few years.

Go back to being open to learning from someone who already has, does or is what you'd like. If they are famous, read their biography – they all have them these days! If you know them, ask them how they do it. Most people will be only too happy to tell you about themselves.

Find out how they motivate themselves, where they draw their energy from and what strategies they have used to get where they are. Then, work out how you can apply those same things to yourself.

If your bike had a puncture, you wouldn't think about what shape 'thing' to replace it with would you? So why reinvent the wheel when you don't have to?

Prepare in Advance

If you find it hard to break into a chain of thoughts and turn them around quickly, one trick I have found works really well is to prepare in advance. Just as you would if you were going to take on a challenge in any other area of your life and as we did earlier in this book when we looked at positive affirmations.

Think of a couple of really happy memories for example and give them a short title (one word if possible) that will allow you to recall them quickly and easily. Spend a few minutes quietly enjoying the memory, recall what you saw, what you could hear and exactly how you were feeling at that time. Immerse yourself in the memory, allowing the sensations, thoughts, sounds and pictures to flood back to you. Repeat your word to yourself as you relive that wonderful time right now and squeeze your fist as you do so.

Then, if you find yourself being sucked into a negative frame of mind, dark thoughts creeping in or you just want to feel better, you can quickly switch those thoughts for your happy memory, just by recalling the word you associated with your memory and squeezing your hand.

If there is a particular negative emotion which seems to plague you, find a memory, or invent a positive scenario in your mind (remember your unconscious doesn't differentiate between real and imaginary) where the overriding emotion is the opposite of the one you are troubled by.

For example, if you often feel sad, pick a time where you felt really happy. If you suffer with guilt, (a very common one) you might choose a time when you felt really proud of yourself; or if fear is a frequent visitor in your world, remember or invent a time when you only felt brave, courageous and determined.

You might like to have a selection of memories ready for different occasions. It's a bit like playing cat and mouse, where you are trying to outwit yourself and break the patterns you have set. It's fun to do and will very soon become a new habit. Taking back control of your thoughts and emotions is one of the most empowering things you can do and the best part is, that you can do it all by yourself, for yourself!

About The Author

Amanda Ball

I am a Master Practitioner of NLP, Time Line Therapy™ and Hypnosis. Helping other people to realise their potential, has been a love of mine for many years. It started as a sideline, then, fed up with the constant grind of the corporate world, I gave up my well paid job in order to pursue this passion.

A year or two on and having tried lots of different things, I am now concentrating on writing and coaching/counselling which I love.

I never get up dreading work anymore, or wondering what kind of reception I'll get at the office. The office is where ever I plug in my laptop now. Favourite offices so far include Budapest, Lanzarote, Andalucia and the South of France!

I am also a proud mother to two fantastic boys, who continue to amaze and delight me and that just about says it all really!

If you'd like to know more, please visit my website, http://julianandamanda.com

JulianandAmanda.com – My Business

JulianandAmanda.com is the name of the company that I now run with my partner Julian.

We understand that the most successful people in all walks of life, whether that be in business, sport or relationships, all first devoted time to their own self development. We realised that helping others with strategies, for both their personal and business development, was a recipe for success and Julianandamanda.com was born.

We now successfully provide coaching and mentoring, in the personal development field, to a growing number of people. We specialise in helping people get their head in the right place, to take their life and business where they really want to go.

We also provide an online library of personal development resources, which is available to everyone. Please feel free to take a look and see if there is anything else which may be of value to you. Why not bookmark our page, or take the RSS feed, to be automatically updated whenever we add something?

....And Lastly

I really hope that you found this book interesting and thought provoking and I hope that you will invest the time in yourself to use the techniques included. I know that if you do, you will really make a positive difference to your own life and to those who are influenced by you.

This book is the first in a series and for more information on the other titles go to http://theselfhelpbible.com

You might like to join me on Facebook at http://facebook.com/theselfhelpbible or follow me on Twitter @selfhelpbible

I am always interested to hear about your views, so please email me at the address below with your comments and feedback.

Thanks for reading and have a great day!

Amanda

Email Amanda: amanda@theselfhelpbible.com

1Time Line Therapy™ is a registered trademark of Tad James, licensed exclusively to the Time Line Therapy™ Association, Inc. Association members in good standing are authorized to used this trade mark in conjunction with their practice of Time Line™ Techniques[i]

Made in the USA
Lexington, KY
12 November 2012